River Rats: Growing Up on the Raritan River

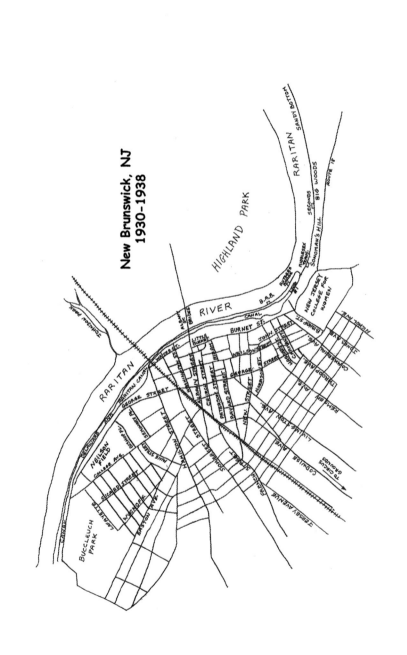

New Brunswick, NJ
1930-1938

River Rats:
Growing Up on the
Raritan River

Alison Hyland

Writers Club Press
San Jose New York Lincoln Shanghai

River Rats: Growing Up on the Raritan River

Writers Club Press
an imprint of iUniverse.com, Inc.

For information address:
iUniverse.com, Inc.
5220 S 16th, Ste. 200
Lincoln, NE 68512
www.iuniverse.com

ISBN: 0-595-14747-X

Printed in the United States of America

To my Daddy with love, Happy 80th Birthday.

Epigraph

The Gods do not deduct from man's allotted span the hours spent in fishing.

—-often quoted by Herbert Hoover

Contents

List of Photos and
Illustrations

Acknowledgements

I wish to thank my former co-workers and friends in the Reference Department at the East Brunswick Public Library for their help in researching the historical background for this book. The Reference Department in my own hometown library of Old Bridge, I wish to thank as well for their assistance. I also wish to thank Yani Siegel for his encouragement and Barbara Lederman for her careful proofreading of the manuscript in its early stages. Mr. David W. Fleming of the New Brunswick Cultural Commission, Inc. for his permission to use the photo of the State Theater. My Mom for the wonderful life-long art training she gave me. Without my sister Aimee's help and encouragement this book might never have come to publication. Most of all, I wish to thank my Dad for enriching my life with his stories of New Brunswick as well as imparting his love of American History.

Introduction

While I was growing up, my father told me stories about his childhood on the Raritan River. It never occurred to me to record his stories until just recently.

One day in early April, Dad and I went down to Sandy Hook to spend the day surf fishing. He cast his line into the water and suddenly yelled, "Hey, Archie and Al went swimming yesterday. Yeah? Where? Down at Sandy Bottom." He laughed and said he was thinking about his childhood on the Raritan River where he and his brother Al liked to go swimming. I knew that story well because I had heard it often. It was then that I realized a book of his memoirs might be of interest to others. When we got home that evening, I handed Dad my microcassette recorder, batteries, five one-hour tapes, and asked him to record his stories. This book, *River Rats: Growing Up on the Raritan River,* is the result.

The following pages are a compilation of true occurrences as seen through the eyes of a boy growing up in a small city on the Raritan River in New Jersey. This is his intimate view of the Great Depression between 1930 to 1938; a time before television, computer games, and the Internet. My father and his friends relied on their ingenuity to provide recreation and entertainment.

My father's memory is vivid and accurate, making him an excellent witness to the 1930s. The people he came in contact with were very colorful, to say the least. They all acquired nicknames that described mannerisms, dress, or lifestyles; even the name River Rats, evolved in this way. I tried to retain Dad's natural, easy way of talking throughout the book. Dad loves American History and I am happy so say that I share his interest. The city of New Brunswick and surrounding areas where Dad grew up, is rich in history. In doing research for this book I found it tempting to write in great detail about the history of New Brunswick; however, I inserted just enough historical background information to add depth to *River Rats*. All the photos on the following pages were hidden in our family attic for over fifty years. Dad remembered each picture in great detail and insisted that they were somewhere in the house. We finally found them. I also included a few illustrations to fill in where photos were not available.

In case younger readers think of trying some of the dangerous stunts my Dad and his friends pulled as boys; let me say this, Dad and his friends were lucky. Unfortunately, a few kids didn't make it. After my dire warning, I hope that you will find my father's stories enjoyable. I certainly enjoyed hearing them while I was growing up.

Happy Reading
Alison Hyland

John Street

"Hey, Archie and Al went swimming yesterday!"

"Yeah? Where?"

"Down at Sandy Bottom."

"No kidding?"

My brother Al and his friend Archie's dip into the Raritan River, at Sandy Bottom, marked the beginning of the summer season for us kids; never mind that it was mid-March.

Every once in a while Mom got excited when she heard about the high levels of pollution in the river.

"I don't want you swimming there," she'd say to us.

"Oh Mom, everybody is swimming in the river. Come on Mom."

"No no, I don't want you swimming there. You don't have bathing suits."

But who needed bathing suits? Of course the guys and I went just the same. I pretty much spent most of my time either on the river or in it when I was a boy. My name is Dan. I was born in 1920 and grew up in a small city in central New Jersey, called New Brunswick.

New Brunswick is located right on the Raritan River. It is anchored on each end by a college with Rutgers University at the northern end of town, and Douglas and Cook Colleges at the southern end. The population of New Brunswick in 1931 was about 34,555. The city was divided up into wards, with the many

1

ethnic groups in town tending to cluster together. One ward was predominantly Irish, while another was Hungarian. My neighborhood, the First Ward, was mostly Jewish. Most of my friends were Jewish; sons of peddlers, storekeepers, and even a Rabbi. We spent a lot of time together on the Raritan River and Delaware and Raritan Canal; swimming and sailing during the warmer months and ice skating during the colder ones. We played ball on the colleges' baseball diamonds, watched Rutgers football games at Neilson's Field, and swiped fruit from the agricultural testing grounds around Cook College.

My father died in 1929 when I was nine years old; my brothers were seven and five at the time. My father had a good job in the city as a movie projectionist; but, typical of many people back then, he didn't take out life insurance. Mom was left with three boys to raise on her own. It must have been particularly difficult because this was during the Great Depression.

During the 1930s there was no such thing as welfare and jobs were scarce, especially for the unskilled. Mom qualified for a small widow's pension that came to about thirty-five dollars a month. She knew how to make her income stretch as did so many people back then. Mom supplemented her small income by working at home cutting out handkerchiefs for an embroidery factory in South River. She made about two to three cents a dozen scalloping the edges. She worked very hard doing this close work all day at the kitchen table, trying to make enough money to feed us and keep us clean. Every week she took a bus into South River, taking in her work to the factory. She came back home with a new bundle of uncut handkerchiefs. Mom did this until I was sixteen years old, when I was old enough to get a full time job to help support the family.

We couldn't afford frills, living on basic meals of soup and sandwiches much of the time. Mom always had a big pot of soup cooking on the stove. My Mom could really make soup: beef vegetable, split pea, chicken soup, whatever she could get to put into the pot. We wore hand me down clothes, and inserted cardboard inner soles into our old shoes. Occasionally Mom managed to buy us some new clothes, but only to be worn on Sundays and special occasions. My aunt had several boys, and one of my cousins was a little older than me, so I got his outgrown clothes.

I didn't grow up in a fancy house. We moved to an upstairs floor in a house on John Street. I didn't mind because we were one block from the Delaware and Raritan Canal and the Raritan River; I thought that was great. After meeting our basic needs of food, heat, clothes, and of course the rent, there wasn't money left for amusements. But let me tell you, kids can be very resourceful. If we didn't have the money to buy the things we wanted, we made them. When my buddies and I got together, we pooled our resources, skills, and imaginations. I have to admit though, if my Mom knew half of the things I did, such as riding ice flows on the river and climbing radio towers, she would have died. I remember my brother Al and I were always whispering to each other, "Don't tell Mom!"

The river and canal provided me with recreation that was both exciting and extremely dangerous. I came in contact with a lot of strange people while living on the river, with names like "Corker Pete," "One Hundred Overcoats," and "One Eyed Beulah." My buddies and I pulled a lot of stupid stunts, caused some mischief, had run-ins with waterfront bullies; while enjoying a free and virtually unsupervised boys life. This book contains my memories as a young River Rat, growing up on the Raritan River from 1930 to 1938, during the Great Depression. New Brunswick and the Raritan River were my home, my playground, and I loved it.

Al on John Street
We lived in a house on John Street, one block
from the D. & R. Canal and the Raritan River.

The Raritan River

The Raritan is a pretty river with winding bends and woods lining its embankments. It is considered the largest river in New Jersey, flowing southeast for seventy-five miles emptying into the Raritan Bay at the lower part of New York Bay. A boat can sail from New Brunswick to New York City, and if continued on course, can reach the Hudson River. It can be treacherous with fast moving currents and unpredictable eddies.

I remember hearing stories about the river from the people who lived there all their lives, and became fascinated with its history. I sailed my boats in pretty much the same place that the Lenni Lenape Indians once paddled their canoes, long before settlers came to America. I played on the same embankments where they fished for black bass and searched for clams. The woods that surrounded the river where I roasted potatoes on a campfire, was once the Indians' hunting grounds.

In the early 1600s settlers came to my part of the Raritan, and later on in that century, a commercial shipping port sprung up with businesses, houses, mills, and taverns. Farm products from surrounding counties of Somerset, Morris, Hunterdon, Sussex, and Warren were loaded onto cargo vessels that lined the docks. The river became an important shipping route, with merchants waiting for goods up and down the New Jersey coast and New York. Later, the shipping routes were extended to New England and as far away as the West Indies. The river was deep enough to allow large sailing cargo vessels to navigate easily in and out of port. New Brunswick became such a successful commercial port that sloops, schooners, shallops, and even whalers constantly lined the docks.

The port of New Brunswick declined in 1834 when the Delaware and Raritan Canal, or D. &. R. Canal as it's sometimes called, was officially opened. The forty-two mile long canal went from New Brunswick to Bordentown. The cargo ultimately went west to open markets in Pennsylvania and beyond.

The D. & R. Canal was considered far superior than the Erie Canal in the mid 1800s. To me, it was my supermarket where I found building materials for my boats, copper wire to sell to junkmen, and empty bottles to sell to the local bootleggers. I must have seen its last few years of operation when the canal was finally closed down one hundred years after its opening. The railroad came in and ended an exciting era in America's commercial history.

Along the canal were over one hundred factories that were built during the mid 1800s. Many of them were still in operation when I was a boy. Of special interest to me was a fireworks factory, our country's first harmonica factory, cigars and cigar box factories, and a copper wire factory.

I remember the Raritan as being very polluted. Many of the old factories along the river dumped chemical wastes into the water back then. Most of the time I never gave the conditions a second thought. You just can't stop kids from having fun, that's for sure.

*View of New Brunswick, Albany Street Bridge,
and the Raritan River*

New Brunswick Natatorium
The Natatorium had diving boards and clean water. It cost twenty-five
cents to swim there.

Sandy Bottom

My brother Al and his friend Archie were usually the first neighborhood kids to go swimming around Sandy Bottom. So, what and where is Sandy Bottom? Well, it's on the Raritan River, one mile south of the D. & R. Canal in New Brunswick.

We had our favorite places to swim, where we spent hours on hot summer days and evenings. One good place was located down at the foot of Sonoman's Hill (locals pronounced it Shin-a-man's), it's just about where the canal started. Rutgers College owned an enormous floating barge where its rowing team kept their shells. The barge had different levels with the lowest being a raft about twenty-five feet long and fifteen feet wide. The students stood on the raft and flipped their boats into the river, jumped in, and rowed away for their practice session. The neighborhood kids found a different use for the raft; we thought it was perfect for diving.

I remember the summers in the city as being very hot. The streets and walks held in the day's heat and didn't really cool down all that much in the evening. There was no such thing as air conditioning in our houses, making it too hot to go upstairs. A bunch of us liked to sit outside till about ten o'clock in the evening. "Hey, let's go swimming," someone would say. Then we'd head down to the river and go to the Rutgers Barge. It was eerie after the darkness set in, pitch-blackness all around us. You couldn't see the water below; it looked like a big black hole. We'd get up on the barge, put our hands out over our heads, and hope we didn't break our necks by hitting a log or something floating below. We'd do that quite often in the summer.

Another good place to swim was called Seconds. Seconds was located about a half mile south of the D. & R. Canal. It was part of a dock once used to tie up boats waiting to be locked through the canal. The dock was constructed of squared off wooden log timbers that lined the bank, creating a low wall. There were rusty metal spikes, oh, I guess about two feet long and one inch square sticking out of the wall. Well, this dock ran for about three-quarters of a mile from the locks down to Sandy Bottom where we went skinny-dipping among a pile of rocks. The rocks were dredged up about one hundred years ago to make the channel for the canal. We'd swim there for a couple of hours, and then when we were just about finished getting dressed, a boat would come along. Of course boats made wake we called rollers. You'd be surprised how quickly we took our clothes off again so we could go swimming against those rollers.

Down the road in the opposite direction, about a one-fourth mile north of the locks, was a wooded area. We liked to go skinny-dipping off the towpath. We called this place B.A.B. (Bare A— Beach). We went there quite often.

We kids looked out for one another; always swimming in a group. If any of us got into trouble, a couple of your friends were there to pull you out. A couple of guys who lived downstairs from us, nicknamed Bomber and Yak, were about five years older than us. My brother Al was about eight at the time and went down to the river with them. Bomber and Yak took off one of their undershirts and put it on Al. They pinned the bottom of the shirt together between his legs making him a bathing suit. They watched Al carefully while they were all swimming. That was neighborhood.

Our swimming areas were hazardous, no doubt about that. Rusty old spikes sticking out of the canal walls and debris always floating along with the tide. The river was treacherous, with fast moving tides and unpredictable current. A lot of the kids who swam down there were ignorant of this, sometimes going too far out. They found it hard to get back again, with the current forcing them farther away from land.

I remember one time a group of kids built a sailboat and took it down to the river. They were inexperienced in sailing and capsized in the swift current. One of the kids couldn't swim. To this day it's still vivid in my mind; all the people, including the kid's father, trying to get him out of the water. When they finally got to him, he was dead. Every year the Raritan claimed lives.

Besides the Raritan, my buddies and I had another favorite place to go swimming called the Clay Pits. This was located off Route 18 South in East Brunswick. We were a little older then, about fourteen or fifteen years old, and needed bicycles to get there. It was once a sand or clay mine. The workmen hit natural springs while digging and water filled the huge pits.

The water in the Clay Pits was a green color from the lime in the soil, but it was a very dangerous place to swim. You'd be swimming around in the water, nice and warm, then suddenly you'd hit a natural spring. The water temperature dropped drastically about twenty to thirty degrees. The banks were slippery from the wet clay and almost impossible to get a foothold. I'm serious about this; a lot of kids died there because they'd get a cramp from the sudden cold and couldn't climb out.

There was a swimming pool in town out on Livingston Avenue called the Natatorium. I don't know how I did it, but somehow I scrounged around and came up with twenty-five cents to go. It was a big pool with diving boards and clean water, definitely safer than either the Raritan or the Clay Pits. I guess it was fun there, but I preferred the river.

Dan on his Bike
We needed bikes to get to the Clay Pits.

Corker Pete

Every summer my buddies and I built a boat. Well, we called those things we built boats. The design was not that of regular boats by any means, they more or less resembled scows.

Somebody, probably one of the old River Rats, explained to me that a scow didn't cut water; it pushed water instead. That explained why it was tough going on the river. We rowed and rowed and never made any headway. Our boats leaked very badly, so badly, that it took two guys to bail out the water while one guy rowed. Somebody, probably another River Rat, told us that when wood gets wet it swells. We believed him and really didn't think much about the building process. The boards we used weren't carefully matched, leaving at least a quarter of an inch gap between them. The wood did swell in the water, but not by much.

Where did we get our wood, nails, and so forth to build our sea-worthy craft? As usual, we scrounged around for our building materials. There were three abandoned houses along the D. & R. Canal where we were able to find fairly decent boards. This big fellow, called Corker Pete watched over them. Oh, he was about six feet tall and weighed close to 200 pounds. Where did he get his name? I really don't know. Well, Corker Pete kept a sharp eye on the abandoned houses. Every once in a while we went into one of those houses to try to find a board. If we went in and Corker Pete was around, he ran us out. We were lucky if we didn't get our butts slapped. That was one place where we got our building materials.

We preferred going down along the D. & R. Canal, our supermarket. We got an awful lot of things from around there, some boards and old rusty nails. During the Depression nails were very hard to come by, so we did the best we could with what we found. We took those bent old nails and straightened them out with a hammer.

No matter how we tried nailing the wood boards together, we just couldn't get them to meet. Our boats leaked so badly that we had to caulk the cracks. The boats sealed up fairly well, so then only one guy was needed to bail out the water while one guy rowed.

We made our own oars from materials we found during our midnight scrounging. A few of our neighbors put up small picket fences around patches of grass in their yards. The pickets were about three and one-half feet long and about one and one-half inches square. Well, one evening we got ourselves a couple of those pickets and nailed part of an orange crate top to each one. They made pretty good oars.

One time we saw a pirate movie and got the idea of building oarlocks. The pirate boats had two pins sticking out, but we didn't know what the pins were made of. Well, they must have been pretty strong to stand the pull of the oars. We tried it. They worked for a while but then the nails came loose and the sticks broke when we were in the middle of the river. We wound up paddling all the way back to shore.

One thing I regret, I never built an iceboat. The winters were really cold in the 1930s. I know we would have used an iceboat quite a lot. I guess we never built one because either we didn't know about them, or never thought about it. If I had known about iceboats, I'm certain I would have built one. That would have been great fun.

Okay, we never built an iceboat, but we did decide to build a kayak. I don't know where we got the idea, but we gave it a try. This was not a one or two guy job, so about five of us got together. Of course we scrounged around for some wood, this time we stayed away from Corker Pete, and went down to the freight yard on the west side of town. The freight yard had some barrel staves lying around. We used the barrel staves for the ribs of the kayak and started to build it. About that time one of my uncles came down and took me to my grandmother's home in Old Bridge.

I was sitting with my grandfather and we were talking, "Well, we will build a kayak," he said. So we did. Grandfather and I walked to South River and got some furring laths, about two inches by one-quarter inches, to make the keel. We found some barrel hoops for ribs, so all we needed was a cover. My grandfather had some muslin feed sacks from turkeys he was raising at the time. My grandmother sewed a couple of them together for us to use as a cover. We nailed the muslin to the frame we had built out of laths and barrel hoops. We finally painted the whole thing. All and all, we made a pretty decent kayak. I don't remember how I got it home, but somehow I did.

The guys and I used that kayak in the Raritan River for quite a while. One day my brother Al rowed it out to the middle of the river. Well, he couldn't get back again because he lost the paddle. He dove out and let the kayak go. He told me he was forced to swim back to shore and just about made it. I believe it, because the river can be pretty swift when the tide is running in. My kayak was lost, but I had a lot of fun building it with my grandfather that summer.

River Rats

Who were the River Rats? Well, that's what the local kids called the people who lived down around the Raritan River, right on the D. & R. Canal. Those guys were related to the river in some way or another, perhaps once children of fishermen, boat builders, or just grew up on the canal when cargo was locked through. They lived around the river their whole lives.

Quite a few of the people around the river lived in boats tied up to the shore along the canal. They weren't big boats, oh, averaging about thirty feet long, and they lived in them all year round. I remember a lock house on the canal where a couple of older men lived. They manned the locks, opening and closing them whenever a boat came through. The canal was still being used when I was a boy but only once or twice a month. Only a couple of men were needed to manage the locks.

Since the locks weren't used much, the men who lived on the river built boats as a sideline. The boats they built for people were usually small rowboats. My good friend Moe and I liked to go down to the canal a lot and watch. They really knew how to build them. Sometimes we were shown around and they talked about their boats, really going into detail. Generally, the old men didn't bother us, and the kids left them alone. In fact they were very good to the local kids and let us take scraps of wood, old nails, tar, or whatever we needed for our projects.

My buddies and I took our leaky boats down to the river on wagons that we also built. The River Rats sat around and watched us struggling with these kids built boats. They'd be chewing tobacco, spit, and say, "Spec't that thing ta'float?" Then they'd chuckle amongst themselves. Well, our boats did float, just barely. I guess you could call us River Rats too, because we were always on the Raritan River or in it most of the time.

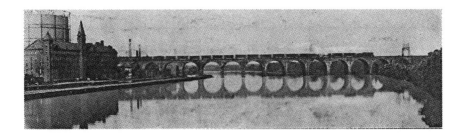

View of the Railroad Bridge and Raritan River
The D.& R. Canal is on the left.

Grandma Allen

The Delaware and Raritan Canal ran parallel to the Raritan River with only a narrow towpath separating them. I lived only one block from the canal so I heard many stories about its early days when it was full of activity.

I must have seen the last few years of the canal's life when I was growing up. I remember it being brackish and stagnant. Only a few boats were locked through, as I said earlier, perhaps once or twice a month at the very most. But, from what I had heard, the D. &. R. Canal rivaled the Erie Canal during the one hundred years it was in full operation.

A local elderly lady, everyone called Grandma Allen, grew up in New Brunswick. She told me stories of the canal days when she was a young girl. To me, the canal was my supermarket; a place where I went junking, scrounging around for copper wire, bottles, old tires, etc. The canal was my favorite ice skating place in the wintertime, and during the summer, the guys and I rowed leaky hand-built boats along its narrow channel. But Grandma Allen had different memories of the canal.

All of us sat on her steps and listened to her as she talked and talked about the history of the canal. I guess she was in her middle to late sixties when I knew her. Now, subtract that number from 1932, and that would bring her childhood to around the 1860s. Grandma Allen said the canal barges started at the first lock, near the foot of Sonoman's Hill. The barges were loaded up with cargo from New York, New England, and other cities along the East

Coast and came up the Raritan River. Wheat and other grains was the original cargo in its early years. Later, coal was the most common cargo to be locked through the canal as it became the major fuel source for many industries in the east. Hundreds of tons of coal came from mines in Pennsylvania and were carried on massive barges along the D. & R. Canal. Finished goods from the east came from the opposite direction and were taken to markets in the west.

The entire length of the canal extended for nearly forty-two miles. It went up through Raritan Landing, around Weston, then back down through Millstone, Black Wells, Griggstown, Kingston, and finally going to Bordentown. The canal was a vital link between New York City as well as other major cities in the east and inland cities in the west. The canal was approximately seventy-five feet wide and about seven feet deep. It was deep enough to permit sloops through, carrying anywhere from seventy-five to one hundred and fifty tons of cargo. According to early records, the D. & R. Canal was more successful than the Erie Canal. It carried more cargo than the Erie Canal, with gate tenders and mule teams working day and night during the peak of its operation from 1859 to the 1860s. Tonnage reached close to two hundred tons per vessel.

It has been a long time since I watched the lock keepers open the canal, but I remember how the system worked at the first lock. Say, a barge that was going out stopped in front of the last gate, a gate in the back would raise and block the canal water from going out into the river. If the river was lower than the water in the canal, which it was most of the time, the forward gate was opened by the lock keeper. They looked like two doors on hinges. The workmen opened a valve that let the water out of the lock until the water level was the same as the river; then, the gates were opened and the barge came out. Coming back, the lock worked just the opposite. The barge came into the lock and the front doors were closed and the back doors were opened. The lock filled up with water until the water level was equal with the river, then the barge continued up the river. Teams of mules and horses were needed to pull the barges down the canal and through the locks. They walked down towpaths that were on both sides of the canal led by workmen, whose jobs it was to make sure the cargo kept moving down the canal. Grandma Allen told us that there were stables in New Brunswick that housed as many as two hundred mules. More than one hundred and fifteen barges passed down the canal in a single day.

Grandma Allen said people lived all along the canal and the river. These people earned their living and supported their families by manning the locks, moving the cargo, and tending the hundreds of horses and mules needed to tow the barges and other vessels along the canal. There was a general store located at the first lock. Grandma Allen said that business was very brisk with people buying supplies for their long journey on the canal. The store didn't have a cash register so the storekeeper took the money he collected and threw it into a large bushel basket on the floor.

The canal started operations about the same time the railroad came in. Eventually, the canal suffered from competition because the railroad was faster and cheaper than the canal. The old general store located at the first lock was no longer there when I was a boy. A few things still remained however, as a reminder of the great canal days.

An old abandoned brick building was still standing on the canal that once had been a bottle-cap plant. I remember a lock house standing up on pilings, nearly ten feet off the ground that housed machinery and materials for the lock keepers. There were a number of canal barges lying on their sides, beached along the timber lined canal walls. After listening to Grandma Allen, I walked around the old canal and I tried to imagine what it was like to have lived there during the mid 1800s.

Poking Around the Old Delaware and Raritan Canal

People threw all kinds of junk around the D. & R. Canal. I liked poking around there because I found materials to build my boats, wagons, and other toys. Occasionally a few very interesting things floated down the canal.

I played ball a lot with my buddies on the Douglas College Campus; NJC it was called then. Sometimes we played ball in Buccleuch Park (locals pronounced it Bugle-low), at the opposite side of town. We found out quickly that kids claimed territories for themselves. We were not welcome at that end of town. Of course we needed balls, but we didn't have the money to buy them. So, how did we get our baseballs?

Guys playing ball at the upper part of town sometimes lost their balls. Rainstorms washed the balls down into the canal; and the catch basin of the city emptied into the canal. Now, we'd go down there and walk around its edge. Better yet, if someone had a boat, we'd row down the canal and pickup the lost balls. There were usually a lot of them; we'd find rubber balls, tennis balls, softballs, and of course, baseballs. So, we always had a good supply of balls to play with. While poking around the canal I saw a few very strange people living down there.

The old barges that were used to haul cargo during the turn of the century were left abandoned along the canal. What could you do with them when they were no longer needed? They were sunk along the edge of the canal in a deep trench. They looked like huge dead monsters lying on their sides. People lived in them, especially the homeless. Back then we called these people bums or derelicts. One derelict I particularly remember was the scroungiest looking thing I ever saw. He had big red watery eyes, long filthy matted hair with a beard to match. Another guy we called "One Hundred Overcoats" lived around there too. I guess he wore every coat he owned on his back.

Besides those characters, quite a few other people lived on the canal; men, women, and married couples, oh, and about four families too. Now, these people who lived on the canal actually lived on the water in boats that were tied up to the inner walls of the canal. I don't imagine they had to pay any kind of storage or docking fee, so they lived rent-free.

I remember the barges were huge; rectangular in shape, about thirty feet long, maybe a bit longer, and twenty-five feet wide. Out of the water they appeared to be ten feet high. Don't forget, they had to be massive in order to haul about 200 tons of coal as well as other heavy cargo down the canal. The barges were constructed of heavy timbers about six inches thick and a foot long. The best description I can give is that they looked like Noah's Ark. Unfortunately, not many survived from the 1800s. The few barges that did survive, can now be found in canal museums.

In the summer, the canal water was filthy and stagnant; a deep trench filled with stinking water. We never went swimming there. The only time the canal was cleaned out was when pleasure boats were locked through, and that was very rarely. Johnson & Johnson Company still used the canal back then. They had a commercial boat that brought in supplies up the river, went through the canal, then to their factory at the north end of town. When the J & J boat came through, it was a big deal to us kids. We always saw dead cats and dogs floating down the canal when the water was released through the locks. Every once in a while a dead human being went floating by too. When a body showed up, there was all sorts of excitement. The canal swarmed with police. The city coroner came down with a panel truck, and then they'd fish out the body and took it away. We thought it was a great place. Well, that's what we thought anyway.

Beached Canal Barge
The abandoned barges were sunk along
the edge of the canal in a deep trench.

Waterfront Bullies

I'll say one thing about the people in my neighborhood, they seldom interfered. We got into arguments as all kids do, and people left us alone. We settled our differences either with fists or rocks, and then later shook hands. We made a lot of noise in the streets and the people were very tolerant, rarely hollering at us.

One thing we liked to do was get ourselves a couple of empty condensed milk cans and stamp down on them. If we stamped on them just right, they folded up and over our shoes. Condensed milk cans were the best because both ends were usually intact with only two holes punched at one end. We ran all around the streets making the worst kind of noise imaginable. The noisier our tin can shoes were, the happier we were. A couple of us liked to go around the corner and stand in front of a stucco house and bounce balls off the side for hours. I hate to think what it sounded like from inside, but the people who lived there never said a word. But once in a while there was someone who was intolerant. Intolerant, that's an understatement!

I'll never forget one time when a few of the guys, about fifteen years old, were sitting around making some noise on our front porch. One fellow, named Ed, had his broken leg in a cast. This man who lived a couple of doors down from my house, came by drunk. Apparently an argument started and the man hit Ed right on his broken leg. I don't know if it was true or not, but Ed said the man hurt him. One of Ed's friends punched the man right in the mouth. The drunk said he was going home to get a gun.

Chaz, Leon, and I were coming home from the movies that evening. When we reached my house the guys were all excited and told us what had happened. I knew this man. He kept his boat tied up on the Raritan River. "Look, he's a fisherman," I warned. "He's pretty tough and might have a gun in his house. You'd better be careful." Well no sooner did my buddies and I go into the house than we heard this loud boom. The fisherman did get his gun and took a shot at the guys outside. Luckily, as soon as they saw the drunk make good on his threat, they ran off. The fisherman found himself a good lawyer and got off, claiming he only shot into the air to scare them. We found out later that bird shot hit one of the cars in front of my house. Fortunately, no one got hurt. The fisherman lived there a little over a year then moved somewhere else.

One kid who lived on the canal, off of Burnet Street, was actually shot to death around 1931 in a similar incident. He had been climbing around on one of the tin roofs, making some noise. A man shot the kid through the upstairs window. The gun was never found and the only witnesses in this case were a couple of kids. The murderer didn't get off, though. He was sentenced to serve about ten years in jail.

When all of us guys were a little older, we had guns. At first we had air rifles and when we got a little older and could afford them, we had .22 rifles. We'd go down along the Raritan River about a mile from Sonoman's Hill, where the bottom of the bluff was, and shoot at cans. A bunch of us got into fistfights just like everybody else, and sometimes we came home with a bloody nose and a black eye; however, we never used guns to settle our arguments.

I guess that every boy has at one time or another come face to face with a town bully. Well, my neighborhood had a bully too. Irving was about a foot taller than I was. He came around pretty often looking for some reason to shove us kids around. One day, we had enough of his bullying. About four of us got together and decided to wait until he came around, then we'd jump him. He came around as expected and we were ready for him. We beat him up pretty good; and as we had hoped, he left us alone for a while. But he came back and if anyone of us were alone, he'd get a hold of the guy and slam him one. I remember one of the guys he hit was the Rabbi's son. We all got together again and jumped Irving for that, but this time he didn't come back.

I didn't see our town bully for about four years. I guess he moved away. I was about 16 when Irving returned. Well, I looked at him and thought, "Hey, he's no bigger than I am." I tried to push this guy into a fight, but he backed off. Just like any other bully, he didn't want to fight a guy his own size. At times, the waterfront along the Raritan River and D. & R. Canal could be a pretty rough place.

"Columbus" and the Farmers Market

During the summer, peddlers came around the neighborhood. Each one specialized in a particular merchandise or service. I remember one peddler sold corn. Now, this corn was not the bi-colored corn you get today. Oh no, it was yellow Bantam corn with large kernels. Another peddler sold fish, while another sharpened knives on a stone wheel and also fixed your umbrellas.

A few of the peddlers were area residents. I remember one peddler who lived at the foot of Burnet Street in a house on the D. & R. Canal. He claimed he discovered a new place to sell his produce. "I'm a discoverer," he bragged. That new place happened to be in South River, only four miles away. Of course the kids latched on to this and called him "Columbus." He resented being called this for some reason. He'd be two blocks away and some kid would say in a normal voice "Columbus discovered America in 1492." I'll tell you, he would chase us kids for blocks. He'd chase us and chase us until he got tired and quit. He was just trying to scare us. Scare a kid? Impossible! But once in a while he caught one and shook him a little, then let him go.

We had a milkman who still delivered milk in a horse drawn wagon. The horse knew the route as well as the milkman. The guy took the milk out of his wagon and went door to door. His horse automatically stopped at every couple houses along the route. The milkman barely set foot in his wagon while making his delivery rounds. We kids thought that was hilarious.

Several junkmen also used horses and wagons to get around town. Of course the horses left manure in the streets. I remember quite a few arguments took place over those piles of horse manure. The neighborhood women waited for the horses to go by then went out to scoop up the stuff to put in their gardens. Each woman claimed rights to the heap on the street directly in front of her house. If a neighbor tried to take someone else's rightful property, an argument started. It was unbelievable.

Down near Sonomon's Hill was a working blacksmith shop, owned and operated by two brothers. They shoed the horses in town. Now that I look back, they were probably the last of the blacksmiths in New Brunswick. Later, when horse drawn wagons were used less and less, and as people owned more cars, the brothers supplemented their income by cutting wood and selling it in wooden barrels.

Many of the storekeepers in New Brunswick started out as peddlers and gradually made enough money to start their own businesses. Their children went on to become professionals: doctors, lawyers, and accountants.

A few of my friends were sons of peddlers. Their fathers bought their produce from the Farmer's Market on Burnet Street, half way between Sonomon's Hill and Albany Street. The peddlers got their fresh cantaloupes, oranges, bananas, cucumbers, and green peppers from the wholesalers and local farmers at the market. The market opened at three o'clock in the early morning and by sunrise, when us kids got up out of bed, it was gone.

My friends told me stories about this Farmer's Market. Well of course kids are curious by nature, and the prospect of a new adventure was too much of a temptation to ignore. So, three or four of us got up enough gumption to investigate the Farmer's

Market. We made a pact that we'd stay up all night and go down there in the morning. My Mom wasn't too happy about it, but I went anyway.

It was pitch black at three o'clock in the morning. I met the guys on a corner and we walked down Burnet Street. It was quite a sight with all the trucks lined up. The wholesalers were there displaying their fresh produce and the local farmers were there too. I'll never forget the smell of fresh fruits and vegetables.

My friend Yankee's father was a peddler. Yankee wasn't his real name. We called each other by street names, or nicknames. Well anyway, Yankee's father gave us a nickel and we went across the street to a Jewish bakery that was also open early. With that nickel we bought four rolls. We went from peddler to peddler; one gave us a tomato, another gave us a green pepper, and if luck would have it, a large onion. We'd slice everything up and put it on our rolls. "Boy, this is real good," we'd say. I can taste it yet.

The police didn't like to see us down there in town that early in the morning. It was okay for Yankee to be there helping his father, but the rest of us were chased away. Of course one visit to the Farmer's Market wasn't enough so we went quite a few times, dodging the police whenever we saw them.

I remember one time we went down there and a cop caught us. We told him we were working for this particular peddler and of course we weren't. The cop went over to the peddler and asked if we were working for him. About fifteen minutes later, the peddler came up. "You boys better go home now because the cops are going to chase you," he said. "One of them asked me if you were working for me, so I thought right away, I didn't want to get you boys into trouble. I said, 'yeah, they help me out a little bit.' So, you better go on home." We went home. Like I said, this was a close neighborhood. Everyone stuck together.

Junkman's Wagon
We knew when the junkmen were coming around the neighborhoods
by the approaching sounds of the trotting horses and jingling cowbells.

Two-Cent Itzsi

Given a choice of playing ball, swimming, ice skating, or going to the movies, the movies was always first choice. During the Depression you could go to the movies for a dime, but money was very hard to come by, if not nonexistent, especially for the kids.

Now, how did we get ten cents to go to the movies? One way was to get the money from our parents. That was pretty tough because parents didn't have ten cents to give to their kids. A dime bought a loaf of bread and twelve cents a quart of milk. A man with a family of three or four, making about thirty dollars a week, wasn't about to hand over ten cents to his kids for a movie.

There were a couple of legitimate ways to get money for the movies, and believe me, we knew them. Along the D. & R. Canal there were quite a few abandoned buildings and sheds. My buddies and I went down along the canal to do some junking; that's what we called it, poking around the buildings and vacant lots. We'd come up with all sorts of great stuff.

Now, at that time, you could get about ten cents for a pound of copper, four cents for a pound of lead; the exact amounts I don't remember. Who took your junk and gave you money in exchange? Why, the junkman. There were three or four of them in the area. Most of our junkmen had their own horse and wagon. This wagon was open with two poles sticking up in front. A strap ran between the two poles with cowbells strung on it. We knew when the junkmen were coming around the neighborhoods by the approaching sounds of the trotting horses and jingling cowbells.

We took all the junk we could find and gave it to the junkmen. He weighed out our stuff and gave us what it was worth: two cents, three cents, four cents, if it was good junk maybe five cents. I particularly remember one junkman who came around quite often. No matter how much junk we gave him he paid us two cents. We called him Two-Cent Itzsi; that's what he gave us, two cents. Kids aren't stupid, believe me, they're not. So, what we did when we had very little junk, we took it to Two-Cent Itzsi. If we had quite a bit of junk, let's say we were fortunate enough to find wire or such, we took it to another junkman. That was another way of getting three cents or four cents. In about a week, if our junking was successful, we had enough money to go to the movies on Saturday.

One junkman incident I'll never forget. It was Halloween somewhere between 1933 to 1934. My friends and I were standing on the corner about nine o'clock at night. We heard this noise and saw a number of guys about seventeen years old pulling a junk wagon out of a shed. They pulled it up Carman Street towards Neilson Street, then northwards to the Albany Street Bridge. I could see it was tough going for them. We didn't think it was right taking someone's property, especially a wagon, the junkman's means of making a living. The guys stealing the wagon were much bigger than us. We were twelve years old at that time and we thought it best not to tangle with them. Well anyway, they pulled and strained until they got the wagon to the middle of the Albany Street Bridge. They worked the wagon up and over the bridge railing, and then threw it into the Raritan River.

I don't know if it was true or not, but the guys said the reason why they took the wagon, was because they saw the junkman being mean to his horse. That was very likely, because as far as I know, the kids in my neighborhood were mischievous, but not to the point of stealing and destroying someone's property.

The junkman ran around the street screaming, "Twenty-five dollars, twenty-five dollars to anybody who can tell me who the kids are who stole my wagon!"

Nobody said a word. The junkman never did find out who the kids were who threw his wagon into the Raritan River. It must have been twenty years later, and you could still see the wagon wheels sticking out of the river when it was low tide.

Albany Street Bridge
At low tide you could see the wagon wheels sticking out of the river.

Neighborhood Bootleggers

Back to our movie money. I loved going to the movies on Saturdays, but like I said, ten cents was hard to come by. Selling junk to the neighborhood junkmen was one way to get a few cents. There was another way; getting money from empty bottles.

There was a nickel deposit on soda bottles. If you found a quart soda bottle of either Hoffman's Gingerale, Canada Dry, or cream soda, you could take it to the local store and get a nickel. If you found two bottles, you went to the movies on Saturday. But, there was another way of getting money for empty bottles; knowing your neighborhood bootleggers.

During the 1930s not only did we have the Great Depression, but we also had Prohibition. The selling, making, and consuming of all alcoholic beverages was illegal. Prohibition at that time was a joke, believe me. I knew for a fact that there were at least four bootleggers who lived in a four-block area. I was ten years old at the time, so you can imagine that if the kids knew who the bootleggers were, so did everyone else.

The family of a buddy of mine owned a house and rented out rooms to a couple of bootleggers. His downstairs tenant was very heavy into bootlegging. Not only did his tenants sell booze, they also manufactured bathtub gin. Now, bathtub gin was made by pouring alcohol into a bathtub then stirring in flavoring and coloring, thereby getting its name bathtub gin. Another bootlegger in the area had a working still. He made Moonshine or White

Lightening, as it's sometimes called. It's known by several colorful names but it all means the same thing, booze.

The bootleggers were always in need of empty bottles and they were willing to pay for them. My buddies and I went poking around the sheds and empty lots down along Burnet Street, on the D. &.R. Canal; there, we'd find empty whiskey bottles. The reason why there were so many bottles lying around those sheds was because some of the guys in town got paid on a Friday night and bought themselves a pint or quart of booze; then, they'd go down to the sheds and drink them.

We'd go down around the canal on a Saturday morning and find the empty bottles. If we found an empty quart bottle, the bootleggers paid two cents. An empty pint bottle brought one cent. So by hook or by crook, and by some maneuvering, we managed to get ten cents to go to the movies.

Once in a while the cops raided our neighborhood bootleggers. Every so often I'd see the police cars pull up to *that* house. The police cars at that time were very old. They were called Paddy Wagons, a little bit bigger than a panel truck with doors that opened in the back. Anybody arrested was put into the wagon. We were always outside doing something, and when we saw the Paddy Wagon come screeching by, we knew that one of our bootleggers was going to be arrested. The police would pull up, then go into the house, and in a few minutes, they'd haul out cases of beer, wine, whiskey, and sometimes even a still.

I can distinctly remember the police bringing out cases of beer and putting them on an old wagon wheel. They took big rocks and smashed up the bottles of beer. All the neighborhood kids stood behind a fence in the next yard to watch the excitement. Sprays of foam shot up like geysers, especially in the summertime when it was hot. When I got home, Mom wanted to know where I was because I smelled like a brewery. Well, all of us kids were sprayed from the beer flying all over when the police smashed the cases. I'd go watch the cops take the owner of the beer out and put him into the Paddy Wagon. He'd be gone for a few days and then be back again. A month later, the kids were selling him empty whiskey bottles to earn money for the movies.

There was another bootlegger who owned a delicatessen. Almost all of the delicatessens were similar around town at that time. The stores were open from seven o'clock in the morning till eleven o'clock at night; selling just about everything. They were very like the convenience stores we have today except that they were privately owned. Mr. S__ openly sold booze across the counter. I knew this because I saw a couple of guys go into his store once to get a few drinks.

Old Mr. S__ was short, round, and smoked a very stubby pipe. I saw the cops put him into the Paddy Wagon during one their raids on his store. He was taken downtown to be arraigned. In a few hours, Mr. S__ was back again and his store open for business.

I remember one time the cops were looking around Mr. S__'s store for booze. They got a tip that he was making it again. A tip, that's a laugh, everyone knew what he was doing. Well, they looked everywhere but couldn't find it. The cops were coming out of the store empty-handed when an eight year old hollered, "Hey, look in the white vinegar bottles." Well, they went back in and looked in the white vinegar bottles. There was the booze. The cops had old Mr. S__ back into the Paddy Wagon. He was gone. It got to a point that more booze was being sold by bootleggers back then than in legitimate beer houses today.

Every kid in the neighborhood knew who the bootleggers were. The eight year old who yelled the booze was in the white vinegar bottles could have been a son of a bootlegger. He was probably eliminating his father's competition. That's the only reason I think he did that, because this was a close neighborhood, and snitching on a neighbor was almost unheard of. Besides, it would have been stupid to ruin the means of earning money for the movies.

The State Theater
We liked going to the movies here because every other show was vaudeville.

Going to the Movies

The movies in town were open on Saturdays. We had blue laws back then, prohibiting theaters from opening on Sundays. As a kid, my whole weekend was not entirely spent out of doors.

Now, there were three movie houses that I went to in town during the 1930s. The State Theater on Livingston Avenue, the Rivoli on the north side of Albany Street, and the Strand Theater on the corner of George and Albany Streets. The fourth movie house was built a little later on Albany Street, fittingly called The Albany.

Like I said earlier, given a choice of things to do on a Saturday, the movies was always first choice. I remember my buddies and I went quite often when we were able to get the money. If you were under sixteen years old you could get into the State or Rivoli for ten cents. We were all about twelve years old, except for our friend Moishe. He took us to the movies but was too old to go to either the State or Rivoli Theater for a dime. So, when Moishe took us, we all went to the Strand.

At the Strand Theater, no matter what your age, you could get in for ten cents. We called the Strand Theater the Old Spit and Whistle. On Saturdays, you could go upstairs and get a movie. Of course they were second-run movies, like Tom Mix, Hoot Gibson, or maybe the Three Stooges. Generally, the Strand ran a feature film, a second run film, and a serial. The serial might be *Tarzan and the Apes* or even *Flash Gordon*. Every week they ran a chapter of the serial, along with a cartoon, and maybe an out of date newsreel.

The movies ran continuously all day from one o'clock in the afternoon to well into the evening, ending at eleven o'clock; unlike the movie houses today, with our feature films staring at one o'clock, then three o'clock, and so forth. The seats at the Strand were generally filled all afternoon. So, we went upstairs and stood up against the projection booth. We stood there until someone left and a seat became empty; then one of us took that seat.

We didn't have money for refreshments; obviously, we barely scraped enough together to get in as it was. Come to think of it, the movie houses didn't sell much in the way of refreshments at that time. We took mason jars full of water with us in case we got thirsty; we were then good for about four to six hours.

Of course being young, we couldn't see the films only once. Oh, no. We couldn't get the whole story the first time around; so, we sat through everything twice. We liked the State Theater because every other show was vaudeville. I can remember sitting through three shows to catch the vaudeville act twice. Mom never hollered too much when I stayed in the theater for almost six hours or more, because she knew where I was. I wasn't getting into any kind of trouble. In fact, she was real happy when I went to the movies on Saturdays.

The Circus is Coming to Town!

"Hey."

"What?"

"The circus is coming to town!"

"No kidding."

"Yeah, clowns and everything."

"How much?"

"It'll cost you a buck to go."

"Oh come on, I can't get a buck, come on."

"What do you mean, we don't pay to get into the circus, we'll go under the tent."

Well that's how we got into the circus. A dollar was a lot of money then, but that didn't stop us from seeing the circus. The walk was a good three miles to the circus grounds from the Raritan River, but we got out there. The circus in town, I just couldn't miss that!

I saw colorful clowns in costume up on stilts, and elephants being watered down by their trainers with long hoses out in the back of the big tent. The strong smell of straw and wild animals mingled with roasted peanuts and popcorn. Bright, colorful lights strung up all around the grounds. Music from the circus calliopes added to the excitement.

My buddies and I had to walk cautiously around the tent because the circus roustabouts routinely patrolled the area just before a performance to prevent kids like us from sneaking under the tent. One of us acted as look out, and if the area was clear, we'd lift up the tent. "Hold it kids," came a voice from inside. There was always some guy up there in the seats telling us to wait because one of the roustabouts was looking our way or maybe someone from the circus was hanging around. As soon as the roustabout turned his back we'd get the all clear. "Come-on kids." You should've seen the kids come flying under the tent, then quickly scatter, blending in with the paying spectators.

One time we unknowingly slipped into seats in the reserved area, only to find out we were the only ones in that section. Let me tell you, we really looked out of place. "Go on kids, get out of here," yelled a roustabout. When he turned his back, we sneaked back in again. Of course he recognized us, "Go on, go on kids." That was the only time we got caught.

One circus I remember well was the Cole Brothers Circus. Clyde Beatty was an animal trainer then, and later, he put together his own circus that travels around today. There were other circuses that came to town, and one in particular was the best of them all.

The really big circus was called the Hagenbeck and Wallace. This was a pretty tough circus to sneak into. A wire fence ran all around the inside perimeter of the tent. We found out the fence was firmly staked to the ground after lifting up the canvas. The fence prevented us from climbing under and getting inside, but we got in.

We figured out that the circus had a place open for the performers to get inside. Well, we found it and slipped in there. I'll never forget that. We saw the Hagenbeck and Wallace Circus! It was a three-ring circus and it was fantastic. If the circus was in town for two nights, we went to see the circus for two nights.

Carnivals were also held out on the circus grounds. They came there about twice a year. We didn't have to sneak in to see those, anyone under sixteen years of age got in free. Even though we didn't have any money, we wandered around the carnival and looked at the colorful lights and listened to the barkers at the sideshows. Unlike the short engagements of the circus, the carnivals stayed in town for about a week. I spent quite a few evenings at the carnival. All the carnivals were alike, it was carnie, it was carnival, and it was a lot of fun.

Dynamiting the Raritan River

Iremember an awful lot of deep freezes during the winters when I was a boy. The stove in our kitchen was our only source of heat in our part of the house. Wouldn't you know we experienced some of the coldest winters on record when I was growing up on John Street? I remember getting up some mornings to find ice on the inside of my bedroom windows. I used to grab my clothes and run for the bathroom that was right off of the kitchen. The stove was close by making the bathroom fairly warm.

Our stove burned coal for fuel and was a combination heating and cooking stove. It had a water tank mounted on the side that provided our hot water. It was my job to get the coal for the stove. Down from where I lived was a coal yard on Burnet and Carman Streets. The coal we bought was called bootleg coal, coming from small coal mines in Pennsylvania. People in town who had their own trucks, went over to Pennsylvania to those family-run mines and loaded up with tons of bootleg coal; then brought it back to sell. Coal was sold in either one hundred-pound sacks or by the ton. When we needed coal, I took my wagon down to the coal yard and loaded it up with a couple of sacks. It was easier for me to take my sled when there was snow and ice on the ground. There was a shed under the porch where we stored our coal. Come to think of it, we never worried about anyone stealing our supply. All the people in my neighborhood were pretty much in the same boat. It was a tough time.

We kept the coal in a coal scuttle near the stove. I was always going down to the shed with that coal scuttle to bring the coal upstairs. The kitchen was the warmest part of the house; so, we used it as our all-purpose room in the winter.

The D. & R. Canal always froze over early in the winter because it was stagnant. The canal was only a block from my house, so I went skating there quite often when the ice got thick enough. The guys and I were always skating if we were lucky enough to get a pair of ice skates. One way or another I was able to get a pair but they were usually hand-me downs. I first tried clamp-on skates but they were rusty and too slow on ice. Luckily, I was given old shoe skates from a relative; but they were too small. Well, that didn't stop me. I cut out the toes so I could fit into them. It didn't matter, I had skates. The guys and I skated up and down the canal. When the river froze, we crossed the towpath and went above the Albany Street Bridge, then over to Highland Park where there was a lake in Johnson's Park.

Ice Skating on the D. & R. Canal was dangerous. The beached barges created a serious hazard in the winter. Most of the stoves in the neighborhood were either coal or wood burning. The poor people who lived in shacks along the Raritan River went out to the canal with saws and cut the wood barges up for firewood to heat their homes. The locals called these people wood hogs. Now, this was the Depression, and people had to survive. Preserving history was not important when families had to be fed and kept warm during harsh winters. After several years of cutting and sawing, all that remained of those huge barges were their skeletons. The massive ribs must have been a foot square and eight feet long, looking like dinosaur teeth protruding a foot or so out of the canal water.

The water didn't freeze well around the exposed ribs of the barges making the ice extremely thin. The water below was about eight to ten feet deep. The locals were well aware of the thin ice and stayed clear of the old barges. Unfortunately, the people from other areas of town sometimes skated too close to the exposed ribs not knowing the dangers. Every year there was at least one person who fell through and went under the ice, then later, fished out dead.

The winters were so cold that even the Raritan River froze over. The depth of the ice ranged from one to three feet thick, and this was tidal water, constantly moving. The ice was thickest at the base of Sonoman's Hill. In the spring, the tides were high from the melting ice and rains. The river melted all right, but it didn't melt quickly enough causing a freshet; that is, tidal water running over the ice. The freshets severely flooded nearby Burnet Street. This happened about every five years with the icy water reaching half way up the block. Burnet Street had a history of floods in the spring; in fact, people had to use rowboats to get down the street.

Well, my town came up with a solution to the severe flooding, minimizing its destruction. The Raritan River was dynamited in the early spring. By breaking up the ice in this way, the water started moving again out to the bay, eventually emptying into the ocean. This was quite a sight. The workmen made holes in the ice and placed dynamite in those holes. We heard loud explosions, Boom, Boom, Boom, echo for miles over the river. Huge geysers of water and spray were seen rising almost one hundred feet into the air.

The dynamiting of the Raritan created ice flows of large thick sheets of ice, roughly six to eight feet square and a foot or more in thickness. We heard cracking sounds as the sheets bumped into each other in the river as the water moved freely along its course. Neighborhood kids, including myself, got on the ice with long poles and rode the flows like rafts around the river. My feet became numb from standing on the ice after only a few minutes. It was a wonder that I didn't lose my footing and slip off into the freezing, fast moving river.

Riding the ice was very stupid. Come to think if it, if any of us fell overboard, we could have died from hypothermia. If we didn't freeze first, I know the moving ice would have definitely crushed us to death.

Middlesex Transportation and the Raritan River
The first lock on the D. & R. Canal is to the left, just above the Middlesex
Transportation building.

Just Hanging Around

There were times when the group of us just hung around the neighborhood. We were never bored; something was always going on and people to watch.

Down at the foot of Sonoman's Hill, just before the first lock on the canal, was Middlesex Transportation. This was a trucking and shipping company with a large warehouse and a dock. Once every summer, a ferry picked up people at the dock in the morning and took them down to the Raritan River over to Coney Island, New York. The vacationers spent the day at Coney Island enjoying its many seaside attractions. In the evening, the ferry brought everyone back to New Brunswick.

One time, the ferry came back but didn't take a pilot on board. The river can be tricky to navigate at low tide. Somehow the ferry left the channel and about thirty feet from land, ran aground on Sandy Bottom. Word spread quickly throughout the neighborhood. You should've seen the people, especially the kids, crowd around the Middlesex Transportation dock to watch. A young fellow named Danny, oh, in his late twenties, found an opportunity to make a few bucks and took his row boat out to the stuck ferry. He charged fifty cents a head to take people back to the Middlesex Transportation Dock. One man on the ferry wanted none of that so he dove off into the water. The water around Sandy Bottom was very shallow at low tide, only three feet deep. He must have landed head first because he was knocked out, apparently, breaking his neck in the dive.

A couple of guys, including Danny, hauled the man out of the water and put him on a door someone found. They carried him, wading through the water, then up a step path and around the bluff to the highway so that the injured man could be taken by car to the hospital. Danny made himself a few bucks that day.

Living so close to Rutgers University the kids were able to take advantage of a very special gift from a generous gentleman. Jimmy Neilson donated a large tract of land on outer George Street. He designated part of this land to be used as a football field. It was fittingly named Neilson's Field. Jimmy Neilson stipulated that there would always be a section for the kids to watch Rutgers football games free of charge. Of course it was near the end zone and the seats in the kid's section were bleachers, but we got to see Rutgers football games the Saturdays in the fall when the team played home. We enjoyed that very much.

New Brunswick was established well before the American Revolution, and many of the old buildings were still standing when I was a boy. On Saturday mornings, during the wintertime, I walked up to the Public Library on Livingston Avenue and went next door to the Guest House. Inside, a woman lit a fire in the fireplace. The kids sat down on the floor in a semi-circle and she read us stories. Now, Henry Guest, a whaler and tanner, built the Guest House in 1760 in another part of town. The house was moved in 1926 to its new location next to the New Brunswick Public Library to escape demolition. I'll never forget the warmth and smell of the wood burning in that old brick fireplace. That was such a simple thing for the library to do, but it meant a lot to the poor kids in the neighborhood. I consider it one of my fondest childhood memories.

Talking about interesting things around New Brunswick, I remember the trolley cars that came down from Milltown along Throop Avenue and down to George Street. One trolley car in particular was brand new. Oh, it was a beauty, black and shiny. This trolley turned into George Street and went down to Albany Street. I remember trying to find myself a nickel to take a ride on it. You know I never did get a ride on that trolley car. I had to be satisfied to watch it go by.

The group of us liked to hang around a delicatessen owned by a man named Joe. He stood out as a very special person in my neighborhood. Joe bought a delicatessen once owned by one of our local bootleggers. He was a nice guy and was a big brother to the bunch of us. We'd go into his store overheated from playing ball.

"Hey Joe, can we have a glass of ice water?"

Joe would reply, "Not until you cool down first."

If things were rough or if anyone of us kids needed somebody to talk to, Joe was always there. If anyone needed a buck, Joe always opened his wallet. One of the kids in my group, who happened to have been an orphan, got into some kind of trouble. Joe went down to the police station to see what he could do. That was Joe. He ran a very successful business for many years. We were always hanging around Joe's store.

A group of us learned to play the harmonica in school. Why not, New Brunswick had the first factory in the country that made harmonicas! I taught myself how to play the guitar too. A group of us would sit in front of Joe's delicatessen; I played the guitar and a couple of the guys played the harmonica. It never failed; a cop usually came around and chased us. He'd yell at us to stop that noise, so we stopped playing our music. When the cop left, we started to play again.

We played ball a lot that's for sure. I told you how we got our balls, but we also needed a bat. Bats were pretty hard to come by, so we had a plan. At that time, Frost Kist ran a promotional campaign. Now, Frost Kist made one of the best chocolate covered ice cream bars ever. Well, Frost Kist had a baseball bat offer, if you got together something like 300 wrappers from their ice-cream, and mailed it in, they sent you a bat. The guys and I couldn't eat 300 ice cream bars, let alone afford to buy a couple of them. What we did, was get a gang of us together and hang around all the delicatessens in the neighborhood. Every time someone threw a Frost Kist wrapper away, one of us ran and picked it up. Eventually, we had enough wrappers collected to mail into Frost Kist and that's how we got our baseball bat.

Hanging around the Raritan River and the D. & R. Canal, I saw some very colorful people; some sly, some harmless, plying their trade quietly around the river. I was naturally curious about everyone who lived around the waterfront. They had a way of talking and dressing that wasn't like the majority of the people that lived in my neighborhood.

No waterfront town is complete without its members of the world's oldest profession. On little Burnet Street, down from the Phoenix Engine Company No. 1, was a house that had a flourishing business. An older friend of mine had a wood cutting business, and he sold wood by the barrel to people in the neighborhood. I occasionally helped him deliver wood to that house near the fire station. You may have guessed it, that was a house of ill repute. We never went inside but we knew what kind of place it was. Nothing was a secret in my town.

Several prostitutes worked in my neighborhood. One was called "Two Bit Liz" who frequented Carman Street along the D. & R. Canal. She got her name for the amount she charged for her services, two bits, or twenty-five cents. I remember one woman was a particularly colorful character.

"One Eyed Beulah" was a big woman with only one eye. Oh, she was really ugly looking. She walked the streets saying hello to everyone she met; people around there knew her by name. She minded her own business, trying to pick up trade up and down Burnet Street. No one really knew who slashed Beulah with a straight razor. A deep scar ran across her right eye, starting at the top of the eyebrow, across her eye, and ending down on the cheek.

I remember one time a woman she knew was weeping and wailing that her husband died, leaving her with several kids to raise on her own. "One Eyed Beulah" came back at her, telling her to go out and hustle. We kids hid behind our hands and laughed amongst ourselves. We knew what was going on. We figured it out for ourselves.

Mischief

Between the ages of nine and fourteen, I had very little adult supervision. There was no such thing as little league, after school clubs, or youth centers. The Boy Scouts was the only organization available to us back then, but it cost money to join; uniform, dues, for starters. Mom couldn't afford it. I was pretty much on my own for finding things to do.

I remember pulling innocent tricks on people in the neighborhood. One trick my buddies and I liked to do was take very very fine wire we found down around the D. & R. Canal. We ran the wire back and forth like a cobweb, between the trees, a porch banister, and a telephone pole. We then sat and waited. People walking down the street ran into our wire, waved their hands in front of their faces, and swore they had walked into a cobweb. We had a good laugh over that.

My town had a dogcatcher. He went around town looking for stray dogs, then when he found one, he put it in his truck that opened in the back. The opening had bars and a screen to keep the dogs inside. This didn't sit too well with the boys in town. We didn't like to see the dogs get caught. One time, the dogcatcher parked his truck in my neighborhood between Commercial Avenue and Carman Street. No sooner than he took off after a dog with his large net, than Mickey came along. Well, he wasn't too happy with the dogcatcher so he went over to the truck and opened the door. He chased a lot of the dogs out that were inside, but he was pretty upset because a couple of them wouldn't get out. "Those stupid dogs," he said, "I'm trying to let them go free and they won't go!"

I remember one time when I came back from visiting my Grandmother in Old Bridge for a few days, I ran into my good friend Moe. His face was all scratched up with deep gouges. I asked what had happened and he said that a couple of Rutgers students came down from the college and paid the kids something like fifty-cents for every cat they found. They wanted a slew of cats for some kind of initiation. Well, Moe went up an alley after a cat and cornered it. The cat came right over the top of him scratching his face and hands. He was a real mess.

I made a lot of my toys. I always had a homemade slingshot sticking out of my back pocket. I suppose sling shots were standard kid's equipment back then. An old rubber inner tube made the best slingshots. Where did I find the rubber? Down by the D. & R. Canal of course. I cut a rubber strip about one and one-quarter inches wide and about a foot long. A leather tongue from an old shoe made a perfect pocket and tied it to the rubber string. I took a stone and placed it in the pocket then pinched the leather together with my thumb and forefinger. Finally, I stretched the rubber by pulling as far as I could, took aim, then let go.

My buddies and I never broke windows with our slingshots. We shot mostly at sign poles, cans, and anything that stood still. I remember the time we were walking along Route 18, about half way between Route 1 and Sonoman's Hill. There were posts along the road with wire fencing running between them. We placed bottles on the posts and tried to shoot them off. There were about five of us that day. Well, one by one we missed. Then Leon grabbed the sling shot and got about three feet away from the bottle.

Leon didn't aim any better than we did. He got off a few shots missing the bottle, but hit a car riding by. I'll never forget that.

The owner of the car screeched on his brakes, got out, and took out after us on foot. Of course we all got out of there fast, and headed down the shill towards the Raritan River. All of us ran except for Tracy, who was a little short fat guy. We called him Tracy because he always said "Mmm, Dick Tracy." He was too slow and got caught. We never ran away from things like that, so all of us went back and explained to the man that we didn't do it deliberately. He had a chance to cool down and let Tracy go, warning us to be careful with our slingshots in the future.

On the corner of John and Hassart Streets was an empty lot. The only structure there was a big billboard. I liked to play on it like monkey bars. When Christmas came around and it was time to get rid of the dried out trees, the guys and I rounded up as many Christmas trees as we could find and took them over to that empty lot. We stacked them high and set the whole thing on fire. Well I'll tell you, the flames from that big pile of old Christmas trees were almost one hundred feet high. It burned and burned. Nobody called the police or firemen; it just burned itself out. We did this every year. It was absolutely amazing.

I became interested in radios when I was about ten years old. My good friend Moe was a radio nut as well. We both started out in electronics by building our own crystal radio sets.

Moe and I liked to walk along the edge of the Raritan River. Sometimes we took a footpath that led up a steep hill. At the very edge of the foot path there was a ten foot drop right into the river. That path took us to the north end of town where Radio Station WJZ had their transmitter at the top of a bluff. They had an antenna up there that was called a wireless. We liked to climb up there to get a good look at the antenna. It's a wonder we didn't fall down into the river, especially after a rain when the wet ground turned slippery.

July 4th was always a big deal for us kids. Somehow Mom always scraped together a dime or a quarter so we could buy some fireworks. During the 1930s fireworks were legal and readily available. New Brunswick had a fireworks factory right on George's Road, at the south end of town. A pack of 150 fireworks cost about a nickel.

I remember one time we were shooting fireworks in the street outside of my home. We saved the ones that didn't go off and set them aside to try again when our supply was gone. I put my bad firecrackers in my shirt pocket. The whole lot of them exploded, blowing off my pocket. I really got burned. One young man who lived next door was studying medicine at the Rutgers Medical School. Barney was his name, a tall fellow who was always studying. If one of the kids got badly hurt, he was there. I can't even count the number of times he treated our cuts and bruises. When the firecrackers went off in my shirt pocket Barney heard the ruckus and came running over and treated my burned chest. He finished medical school and became a very good doctor. The kids in the neighborhood gave him quite a bit of experience to be sure. Years later, when the U.S. entered World War II, he enlisted in the Navy as did my two younger brothers. My Mom was so worried. Barney said to my Mom, "Don't worry Mrs. Hyland, if I come across your boys I'll look after them."

After the war he became a well-known Hollywood doctor. I swear, I lived a charmed life to have made it through my childhood.

Clubhouse on Fire

My brother Al and his friend Archie always built a clubhouse in the late fall. They wanted a place to sit, sheltered from the cold evenings, and bat the breeze with their friends till about ten o'clock at night.

Usually they built the clubhouses in Archie's backyard. They were rude constructions, typical of what you would expect a couple of kids to hammer together. During their midnight requisitions they found wood from abandoned old houses in the area. Sometimes they scrounged materials from peddlers down along the canal.

Al and Archie decided they needed a light for their clubhouse. They searched around and found a black ball around eight inches in diameter with a wick on top. The best way I can explain it is that it looked like a round black bomb. It gave off thick black smoke to warn people that there was a hole in the road. Well, Archie and Al borrowed one of those things and put it in their clubhouse. The only problem was that it was too smoky, so they had to scrounge around a little bit more. They found a lantern hanging on wooden horses that were blocking a big hole in the road. Archie and Al grabbed it one night and ran up the street. They tried to blow out the light so nobody knew they were taking it. Of course the lantern was built so that it wouldn't go out in the wind. The two kids got the lantern back to their clubhouse without getting caught. I realize that we were no angels when we were kids, but the people in our neighborhood didn't mind much.

The weather was starting to get cold one fall; so Al, Archie, and three of their friends decided it was time to build their annual clubhouse. They picked a different location instead of Archie's backyard that year. Al and his friends found themselves a building site on a vacant lot. The lot was on Commercial Avenue, halfway between John and Burnet Streets, next to a car repair garage. Next they needed building materials.

They went down to the canal to scrounge around. People used the canal for a dump. I don't mean a filthy dump with heaps of trash, but a dumping site for old tires, pans, huge drums, etc. An old man named Mose, was a rigger and lived on the canal. He stored a lot of things down there: pumps, rope, even a wet grinding stone we used once in awhile to sharpen our knives. Well, Mose had a rack body from an old truck thrown in a heap. This was a frame made out of wood slats. The corners were reinforced with iron braces. The kids asked the old rigger if they could have it for their clubhouse. Mose said to go ahead, take it. Later, he told somebody that he would rather give it to the kids than have them steal it.

Al and his friends took the rack body and put it against the garage with one corner up against a fence. They covered the thing with whatever they could find such as tarpaper and cardboard. The weather was getting cold so they needed to come up with a makeshift stove to heat their clubhouse. Again, they went down to the canal and took back with them one of the empty twenty-five gallon metal drums that were lying around. They cut a door in the drum with a can opener and cut a hole in the top. Somebody's drainpipe or down spout made a nice chimney. They wound up with a fairly decent working wood stove.

The kids lit a fire in the stove, and let me remind you, the red-hot chimney came out of the rack body and through the tarpaper and cardboard. Well, you can guess what happened next. The cardboard caught on fire with everything going up quickly in flames. I was coming back from the movies with Chaz and Leon when we heard fire sirens. We looked down Burnet Street and saw flames and smoke. The fire was going pretty good when we got there. I saw Al and his friends standing around watching the firemen trying to put it out. "Uh oh," I said, "the kid's clubhouse went up."

I'll tell you, the firemen were pretty mad that some kids' clubhouse caught on fire right next to a building. Luckily, the garage was made out of stucco and didn't go right up along with it. The angry fireman swung his ax to knock the clubhouse down. The rack body had iron corners and I can still hear that ax bouncing off the iron frame. Finally, the entire structure was torn apart. "Who belongs to this?" shouted the fireman. Nobody knew anything. The firemen never did find out it was my brother Al and his friends.

Al and Archie's Clubhouse
The clubhouse was built out of an old truck's rack body,
and covered with cardboard and tarpaper.

Dan and Friend at Antilles Field
Antilles Field was surrounded by a three foot wall made of decorative
brick.

Free Lunch

One thing I was able to get as a boy and can't get now, is a really good loaf of rye bread. The closest thing I can get today is a sour rye bread, but it still isn't the same.

There was a bakery on Burnet Street that made a loaf of rye bread that was fantastic. It was about two and one-half feet long and eight inches in diameter. The storekeeper cut one of those loaves in half for me, because a full loaf was too much. He weighed it and charged me accordingly. I took my half loaf home and put butter on it. Now, this was real butter, not the kind you get in sticks today. Mom bought the butter from the A&P, and the clerk there scooped out the butter from a huge tub and weighed it. Let me tell you, that rye bread smothered with tub butter was a meal in itself. It was real good.

If I got a nickel, sometimes I went to the deli where they sold ice cream. The deli also sold kosher pickles for a nickel. They were almost a full cucumber in size; crunchy, sour, and full of garlic. Oh, really good. It took me a full ten minutes to decide if I wanted to buy an ice cream or a kosher pickle. Sometimes the pickle won out; sometimes the ice cream.

I hear so much about good nutrition and kids today. Many times the only thing we had for lunch and supper were tomato sandwiches and vegetable soup. Mom did her best to put food on the table, but growing boys are always eating. So, my buddies and I found ways of getting a free lunch.

Cook College, the agricultural college of Rutgers University, was located a few miles south of NJC, across from Route 1. When I was a boy, Cook did a lot of experimenting with grafting fruit trees and growing new varieties of vegetables.

The college grew peaches the size of cantaloupes, big ox-heart cherries almost as large a plums, and pears that were very sweet. We climbed the fences that surrounded the experimental fields and groves. If the groundskeeper didn't chase us, we came away with some of the fruit. He probably chased the kids away because they broke the limbs on the trees. We had other ways of getting a free lunch as well.

NJC held a picnic for its students and parents every year on Antilles Field. A big barbecue was set up with grills going all afternoon cooking hamburgers and hot dogs. Of course the kids wanted some of the food.

Antilles field was almost the length of a football field, surrounded by a wall made of decorative brick about three feet high. Kids can climb, that's for sure. We had no problem scaling that wall. The college paid a watchman to look after the grounds. He was about, oh, in his sixties and retired. If he saw any kids, it was his job to chase them away.

Kids are quite good at devising plans, especially when they want something. We split ourselves up into two groups. One bunch of us came up on one side of the brick wall, and while the watchman was chasing us, the second bunch came piling up and over the wall at the other end. Once we got inside the field, it wasn't too bad. I don't think anyone thought that those rag-a-muffin kids belonged to the college parents; but no one said anything about us being there. We walked over to the barbecue and got ourselves some hot dogs, hamburgers, and a bottle of soda. We went back two or three times. No one chased us away, so we had a great time.

We were always walking up to NJC to play ball on their baseball diamonds. Sometimes we were gone for four to five hours. Now, all that ball playing made us thirsty. We had a trick for getting a drink from the watering system on the grounds.

There were pipes sticking out of the ground with faucets on them. I guess a sprinkling system was attached to the pipes to water the grass. The handles to the faucets were always gone, probably removed by the groundskeepers so no one would take them. Well, one of us found a handle that fit those faucets. We carried it with us all the time when we walked over to the college. When we got thirsty, one of us attached the faucet and we all got a drink of water. We did that all the time.

Down along the Raritan River there was a place we called the Big Woods. The Big Woods had a lot of trees, and ran from the foot of Sonoman's Hill over to about where Route 1 is today. A little further down and it turned into swamps. The guys and I took some potatoes down to the Big Woods and made Burnt Micks. We built a fire over some coals and allowed the coals to get real hot. Then we threw in the potatoes and left them in there for quite a while. The potatoes were burnt on the outside and half-raw on the inside. Boy, they were good. Now where did we get the potatoes?

There was a deli on the corner of John and Hassart Streets. The door opened at an angle and had a big porch. The store itself was very small inside, so the storekeeper put a lot of his produce out on the front steps. He generally put out one hundred pound bags of potatoes. That was a mistake. A group of us causally sat on the step and leaned up against the wall. One guy put his hands in the bag of potatoes and passed one at a time to the next guy. He passed the potato on to the next, and so forth, until we decided we better get out of there. Then, we headed out to the Big Woods to have ourselves a Burnt Mick roast. I don't know why the storekeeper never got wise to us. Maybe he did and let us get away with it. I don't know. Like I said, we were not angels.

Cigar Box Factory
Scraps of mahogany were thrown in a pile in back of the Cigar Box Factory.

Regattas on the Raritan River

I was in my middle teens when I started working. My best friend Moe and I scraped enough money together to buy an outboard motor from Sears and Roebuck. We bought a boat from a couple of kids that turned out to be too big for us to handle.

By this time our boat building skills had improved, so we cut the boat down and pulled the stern in a little bit. We fitted the outboard to it and we took our boat out onto the river. Oh, by the way, this one didn't leak.

One time Moe and I took our boat to Staten Island, New York. Now, if you run down the Raritan far enough, and stay on course, you will come out on the Hudson River. That was an all day trip. We enjoyed it, although it got a little monotonous after we passed the interesting factories on the Raritan. That boat was one of several we owned while we grew up together.

Down along the D. & R. Canal and Raritan River were quite a few factories. One factory made wooden cigar boxes. The wood that was used to make the boxes was of a very nice quality; fine grained and nice smelling. I believe it was mahogany. Now, if you went down around the Cigar Box Factory there were scraps of wood strips about one-eighth inch thick, three-quarter inches wide, and from eight to ten feet long just thrown in a pile. I remember one guy who lived on the canal, built a canoe out of those mahogany strips. It was beautiful. Somehow Moe and I bought the mahogany canoe from the builder with birthday money we were given. He only asked a couple of bucks for all his work, then we found out why; it was very heavy. Getting it over to the river was next to impossible.

I was a skinny kid back then and Moe wasn't that much bigger. This canoe we bought was too heavy for the both of us. So we got together a couple of the guys and we all tried to pull this thing across the canal towpath. It took quite a bit of work then realized that we couldn't do it. Neither Moe nor I had the money for a boat trailer. We remembered seeing some of the old timers solve a similar problem. They used a roller method.

We used rollers to get our boat over to the river, a fairly simple solution. We found some pretty heavy round bottles and used them. This was the trick: we put the bow of the boat on the tow-path and pulled it to about one-third of the way. We placed a bot-tle under it and rolled the boat about two-thirds of the way and put another bottle down. We kept doing this until the boat reached the river's edge. The River Rats stood around watching, amused by the whole thing. I guess they had nothing better to do.

The roller method worked so we were able to get our boat into the water. Moe and I paddled down the Raritan to Crab Island, almost into the Raritan Bay. We paddled down and back again. I remember my hands were raw for quite a while because we pad-dled down when the tide was coming in and back when the tide was running out; so, we bucked the tide each way. I guess that wasn't very smart, but we went ahead anyway. Talk about doing things the hard way. Well, I guess Moe and I were masters at that.

At least a couple times a month, on Sundays, a Regatta was held on the Raritan River. Almost everybody who had a boat or liked boats came to watch. People lined up on the river embank-ment or on their boats, if they had one, to watch the speed boat races and canoe fights. There were competitions between a couple of guys in canoes. Each one held a long pole with some sort of boxing glove securely attached at the end. They fought each other until one guy was knocked into the water.

One time there was a special regatta, celebrating some kind of anniversary. All the boats in the river and yachts from a marina in Highland Park were all lit up with bright lights. The fancier boats passed a review stand that was set up on the Rutgers racing team's raft at the base of Sonoman's Hill.

Moe and I had a small rowboat at that time with our outboard motor from Sears and Roebuck we called the Putt Putt. We contemplated going in line with the yachts and pass the judges' stand. We never did, but that would have been great.

Moe and I ran that outboard motor for, I guess, three more years then quit when Moe went into the service. Al and Archie took it over and ran it for a few years more. As a matter of fact, I still have it in my cellar. We had a lot of fun with that outboard.

Dan on Crab Island with Putt Putt
Moe and I had a small rowboat with an outboard motor
from Sears and Roebuck we called the Putt Putt.

Fishing

My brother Al and I loved to go fishing. Living only a block away from the Raritan River anyone might think that I could simply throw my fishing line right out my bedroom window and haul in a fish. Unfortunately, there wasn't much fishing in the river when I was a boy.

The river was loaded with fish and clams when the Indians lived here some hundreds of years ago, but the Raritan I knew was dirty and too polluted to do any fishing. The New Jersey Department of Health later reported that there was a major clean-up of the rivers in the state. The Raritan was one of the rivers greatly cleaned up of pollutants, making it safer for bathing. I was glad to hear that because it's a beautiful river, and I spent many happy hours on it with my friends.

Weston's Mill was one of our favorite fishing spots. About a hundred years ago it was one of several mill towns built on streams that fed into the Raritan, and later, became the watershed for the city of New Brunswick. No one was allowed to take a motor boat on the water because it was our water supply. Rowboats were permitted there and the fishing was pretty good.

Al and I took a few hot dogs with us and spent the entire day fishing. Weston's Mill had quite a few varieties of pan fish; such as, sun fish, perch, bass, and calico. I remember my brother caught some kind of bug with funny looking wings and put it on the hook to see what might happen. Well, he caught a black bass, so big that it wouldn't fit in Mom's dishpan.

Another place I liked to go fishing was south of town where a creek emptied into the Raritan River. Moe and I had gone there with our boat to try some crabbing for a change. There were crabs in that creek all right. We caught a quarter of a bushel basket of them. When we got home we didn't know what to do with our catch. I didn't like crab at all and Moe wasn't too keen about eating them either. One of the River Rats stopped us and gave each one of us a half a buck for the whole lot. Oh, we probably got gypped but that was beside the point; we had a nice day.

I fished a lot when I was a boy, even when I didn't have a boat. I'd stand on the embankment at one of my favorite fishing holes and fished all day long. I believe I didn't get into too much trouble as a kid because I was either on the river or fishing most of the time. When kids are fishing, they aren't getting into trouble.

When I look back, a lot of things could have been nicer, perhaps better food and warmer clothes. Actually, I was never sorry the way I was brought up or the neighborhood I lived in. Everyone looked out for one another. We were a close-knit community, from the old River Rats keeping an eye on us on the Raritan River to the neighborhood peddlers and storekeepers in town. The Raritan River, Delaware and Raritan Canal, and the city of New Brunswick were my home and my playground. My childhood memories are very special to me; they are of another era, of another time.

New Brunswick Water Works-Our Favorite Fishing Hole
Motor boats were not permitted here because
it supplied water to the city of New Brunswick.

Afterword

If you are curious as to what became of my father after he left New Brunswick, Dad went from building leaky boats as a young boy to building highly sophisticated spacecraft as an Engineering Technician for RCA's Aerospace Division. If you get a chance to go to Washington DC, pay a visit to the National Air and Space Museum. On display, you will see two of our Nation's earliest satellites, Tiros and Itos. Dad's fingerprints are all over them. Those are two of many projects he worked on during the height of America's space program. As a side note, you may be interested to know that seven out of ten young River Rats from Dad's neighborhood joined the U.S. Navy during World War II. Corker Pete lived to be 101 years old.

Dad and I recently took a ride into New Brunswick and much has changed from the 1930s. Sonoman's Hill is still there but only a fraction of its original size. The D. & R. Canal has been restored and is now a living museum. The spring freshets no longer flood the lower parts of New Brunswick. The buildings along Burnet and John Streets, including Dad's home, were demolished to make way for the new Route 18. Downtown New Brunswick's main thoroughfare, George Street, has been revitalized, complete with cobblestone street. The State Theater has been renovated and is now a splendid theater where big names come to perform. But there is one thing that has not changed, the beauty of the Raritan River.

About the Author

Alison Hyland holds a BA degree in Art from Thomas A. Edison College with undergraduate work at Rutgers University, Open University. She attended the Graduate School of Education at Rutgers University, and worked towards a Masters Degree through the State University of California with a concentration in history. She plans to complete her Ph.D. in Humanities.

Alison studied illustration under internationally known illustrator Steven Kidd at the Art Students League in New York City. She completed intensive art training with pastel painter, Ernest Savage through Sir Isaac Pitman College, London, England. She worked as a Graphic Designer and taught painting in evening school for over seven years.

Alison is single and currently lives in Old Bridge, New Jersey where she is a Webdesigner. She is the daughter of artist Doris Hyland.

Bibliography

Barber, John W., assisted by Henry Howe. *Historical Collections of New Jersey: Past and Present*. Spartenburg, SC: The Reprint Company, 1975.

Beck, Henry Charlton. *The Jersey Midlands*. New Brunswick, NJ: Rutgers University Press, 1984.

Cawley, James and Margaret Cawley. *Along the Delaware and Raritan Canal*. Cranbury, NJ: Associated University Press, Inc., Fairleigh Dickenson University Press, 1970.

Cunningham, John T. *This is New Jersey*. New Brunswick, NJ: Rutgers University Press, 1978.

Decks, Scott, ed. *The Value of a Dollar 1860-1989*. Detroit, MI: Gail Research, Inc., 1994.

Federal Writers Project, Works Progress Administration of New Jersey. *New Jersey 1838-1938*. New York: Viking Press, 1938.

Illustrated Official Book of New Brunswick, New Jersey. New Brunswick, NJ: Thatcher-Anderson Co., 1931.

Kross, Peter. *New Jersey History*. Wilmington, DE: the Middle Atlantic Press, 1987.

Levitt, James H. *For Want of Trade*. Newark, NJ: The New Jersey Historical Society, 1981.

Meuly, Walter C. *History of Piscataway Township 1666-1976*. Somerville, NJ: Somerset Press, Inc., 1976.

Myers, William S., ed. *The Story of New Jersey*. New York: Lewis Historical Publishing Company, Inc., 1945.

Patt, Ruth Marcu. *The Jewish Scene in New Jersey's Raritan Valley 1698-1948*. New Brunswick, NJ: Jewish Historical Society of Raritan Valley, 1978.

CPSIA information can be obtained at www.ICGtesting.com
Printed in the USA
BVOW082042130313

315493BV00003B/305/A

9 780595 147472